## Bibi Lucille

Bibi is an award-winning actress, having won the Starnow award for Rising Star and the Women of the Future award (2021) for her contribution to Arts and Culture. She studied acting at Questor's Youth Theatre in Ealing before beginning her professional career at the age of 19 with a lead role in Noel Coward's 'This Was a Man' in the West End. She returned to Leicester Square Theatre for a lead role in 'Lipstick and Scones' before a month-long run at the Edinburgh Fringe. Other roles include Lady Anne in 'Richard III' (Baron's Court) and Jane Watson in the UK tour of 'Hound of the Baskervilles' (London Mayor's Choice 2018).

Screen credits include: 'All Inclusive' which won first prize at the 48hr Sci-Fi Film Festival and garnered Bibi a 'Best Actress' nomination at the Pastel Film Festival. She then went on to star in PopstarTV!'s 'Purgatory' and Amazon Prime's 'Trust'. She gained a cult following from the indie web-series 'I Am Sophie' which won first prize at the BAFTA and Oscar-qualifying Flicker's RIFF film festival.

Following the pandemic, Lucille began writing her first play, 'Meat Cute'. Following its debut at The Chiswick Playhouse and Camden Fringe, the play gained critical acclaim and became a finalist at the Offest Awards.

First published in the UK in 2023 by Aurora Metro Publications Ltd
80 Hill Rise, Richmond, TW10 6UB
www.aurorametro.com    info@aurorametro.com
twitter @aurorametro FB/AuroraMetroBooks

Printed on sustainably resourced paper.
ISBN: 978-1-912430-97-0 (print)
ISBN: 978-1-912430-98-7 (ebook)

# Meat Cute

## Bibi Lucille

AURORA METRO BOOKS

# CONTENTS

# Patch Productions

Founded in 2020 by Anastasia Bunce and Maria Majewska, Patch Plays is a theatre company devoted to staging new writing that explores environmental sustainability, animal welfare and their intricate connection. The company is focussed on telling entertaining personal stories to engage audiences with these themes, to challenge and provoke empathy, whilst also offering hope for a better future.

Established in 2020, the company has since produced three plays including 'Meat Cute' by Bibi Lucille (Gilded Balloon, Edinburgh Fringe Festival 2023, Vault Festival 2023, Chiswick Playhouse, Bread and Roses, Hen and Chickens as part of the Camden Fringe 2021), 'Blood On Your Hands' by Grace Joy Howarth (Cockpit 2022) and 'Birdie's Adventures in the Animal Kingdom' by Grace Joy Howarth (Greenhouse Theatre 2023 and Harrow Arts Centre 2022).

*Meat Cute* was first performed as a ten-minute short for Patch Play's scratch night at the Tide Tables Cafe, Richmond, in October 2020. It went on to debut as a full play at the Chiswick Playhouse in May 2021.

## Cast

Writer/Performer – Bibi Lucille

## Creative Team

Director/Producer – Anastasia Bunce

Dramaturg – Anastasia Bunce

UU Xinyou Zhang – Associate Producer

A.T. – Executive Producer

Flick Isaac-Chilton – Sound Designer

Gabriel Saint-Hampton – Choreographer

Chiara Fulgoni – Photographer

Acknowledgements:

With thanks to Kim and Robert Salmons, Dusty Salmons, Anna Barkan, Stuart Bunce, Chiara Fulgoni, Ashley Bowman, Mohammed Patel, Rachel Thomas, Flick Isaac-Chilton, Bella Glanville.

Tide Tables Cafe, Bread and Roses Theatre, Hen and Chickens, VAULT Festival, Book on theRise, and to all our friends who have continually rooted for and supported us since 2020 with the development of the show.

# BIOGRAPHIES

### Anastasia Bunce – Director and Producer

Anastasia Bunce is a theatre and film director based in London who directs new plays and modern classics. Anastasia is the Artistic Director of Patch Plays, a company devoted to staging new work that explores animal ethics and sustainability. Anastasia trained in Theatre Directing at Mountview Academy of Theatre Arts in 2020. Stylistically, she is interested in utilising expressionistic devices that enable the poetry of a piece to become its focal point, as this for her, is where stories shape into art.

Credits include the critically acclaimed (**** *The Stage)* 'Darkie Armo Girl' by Karine Bedrossian (Finborough Theatre 2022), 'Meat Cute' (Gilded Balloon 2023, Vault Festival 2023, Chiswick Playhouse, The Hen and Chickens for the Camden Fringe and The Bread and Roses Theatre 2021), 'Blood On Your Hands' by Grace Joy Howarth (Cockpit Theatre 2022), 'Summer and Smoke' by Tennessee Williams (Exeter Phoenix, 2017), 'Plucked' (Space on the Mile, Edinburgh Fringe 2018) and 'Birdie's Adventures in the Animal Kingdom' by Grace Joy Howarth (Harrow Arts Centre 2022).

Film credits include 'Meat Cute' by Bibi Lucille (2023), 'Yoghurt is Not Sexy' by Jessica Friend (2021), 'Swipe Left' by Bella Glanville (2021) and award-winning 'Push' by Julia Melinek (2022).

### UU Xinyou Zhang – Associate Producer

UU Xinyou Zhang is a London-based theatre producer who focuses on new writing that addresses the topics of immigration, asian and minority groups, and social issues. Zhang trained in MA Musical Theatre (Producing) at Goldsmiths, University of London in 2021. Zhang's experience in producing includes musicals, theatre, live events and community festivals.

Recent credits:

'The Pudding Club' (Cage, Vault Festival 2023), 'Walking Cats' (Network Theatre, Vault Festival 2023), 'The Pudding Club' (Cage, Vault Festival 2023), 'Passing Through Every Part of the Brain (Crypt Galley, 2022), 'FeastFest Festival' (support by Royal Docks team, 2022), 'Blood On Your Hands' (Cockpit Theatre, 2022), 'There's A Dead Body in my Living Room' (Etcrate Theatre, Camden Fringe Festival 2022), 'Hill Behind the Hill' (Seven Dials Playhouse, 2021)

## Flick Isaac-Chilton – Sound Designer

Flick is a musician and theatre professional, who trained at the Guildhall School of Music and Drama, and Mountview Academy of Theatre Arts. She has performed at the Shaftesbury, Savoy and Adelphi Theatres, the Royal Albert Hall, Barbican, Arcola, Southwark Playhouse, Soho Theatre, The Other Palace, ATG Aylesbury Waterside and has recorded for Broadway On Demand.

As a sound designer and composer, she has worked on 'Meat Cute' (Chiswick Playhouse, Vault Festival 2021-23), 'Hanging Around' (The Pleasance 2023), '12.37' (Finborough 2022), 'I Am Turpin' and 'Salomé' (Theatre N16 2016-2017), 'A Little Princess' (Edinburgh Festival Fringe 2016), 'And Eve?' and '[redacted]' (Catalyst 2020) and 'As Happy as a God in France' (Burgh House 2023).

# PREFACE

## Bibi Lucille

In January 2020 the virus we now know as Covid made its evolutionary jump from animal to human. The official line is that it achieved that deadly leap in a wet-food market that traded – for human consumption – dogs, racoons and bamboo rats. In my small corner of the world, I found myself unemployed. Alongside millions of others. Acting was my lifeline and any writing I had done remained in a folder on my laptop, intensely labelled as 'PRIVATE' in capital letters. Never to be seen or experienced by anyone other than myself.

That all changed during a wine-fuelled and socially distanced evening with my cousin (and future director), Annie. She asked me to write a ten minute piece for a vegan themed scratch night. I drunkenly asked her, 'what would I even write about?'

'What if you write about the way you eventually turn all your boyfriends vegan?' she said, taking a final, satisfied gulp of alcohol. The next morning at 5am, my mouth dry and my head pounding, I had a sudden spark of inspiration. Sitting up in bed I grabbed my phone, opened the Notes App and started typing. Three hours later, the dawn chorus was over and the first ten minutes of 'Meat Cute' was born.

I have had an inexplicable love for animals from a young age. Their innocence, curiosity and surprising understanding had always fascinated and endeared me. Raised a vegetarian by my mother (overlooking the brief, panicked interlude when she fed me sliced ham because she thought I was too short for my age), I soon decided veganism was the most ethical way I could exist. It wasn't easy. Having been raised on pasta and cheese, it took me three years to give up the dairy, but at seventeen, I made the commitment. Becoming vegan opened up a world of questions, trials, tribulations and confusion, mainly from restaurant waiters taking my order, and bemused family friends wondering if I had an eating disorder. The act of caring deeply for a cause that feels so completely out of your control fuels a lot of anger. Unfortunately, the anger was only hurting myself; I realised how futile it was trying to convince people to put down the bacon; while throwing my sister's animal-tested shampoo across the room and cracking a window, wasn't winning me any friends.

Fusing my love for comedy and my debilitating passion for animal rights finally felt, at best, enlightening. To be engaging, enjoyable, convincing and most importantly, listened to. Fighting for a cause that is so wildly out of your control can feel like screaming into the pit-less abyss. The voice of an activist is the one that screams the loudest but feels the least heard. Not only does *Meat Cute* address the V-word, it aims to tell the story of an activist and to explore the reality of what it means to care in a seemingly indifferent world.

This play is for everyone. The vegans, non-vegans, the activists, the comedy lovers. *Meat Cute* is the tale of a woman desperately trying to change the world, one tinder date at a time.

# MEAT CUTE

### by

### Bibi Lucille

## Characters

**LENA**

*This play is intended to be performed as a one-person play but could be performed by a group of actors. Other characters portrayed in the play:*

**(TOM)**

**(CHAD)**

**(WAITER)**

**(SPARROW)**

**(DOLORES)**

**(CHRIS)**

**(MUM)**

**(DAVID)**

**(STEPHEN)**

**(DAD)**

**(TARQUIN)**

**(DANIEL)**

**(BLOND GUY)**

**(SIX)**

**(SOPHIE)**

**(DRIVER)**

## Scene 1. A succession of dates.

*A woman stumbles on to the stage, searching for a bucket to throw up into.*

LENA          I need to stop getting drunk. I woke up this morning for the third time this week with that sick kind of alcohol-fuelled feeling in your stomach. The one where you need to run to the loo and then marvel at how skinny-slash-bloated you look in the mirror.

Last night was my third date this week so I was feeling pretty good about myself. It was nice. He was nice. He made me laugh. He spent 40 quid on four tequila shots *and* two G+Ts... he was well-built, you know, not in the gross looks-like-a-walking-cloud way but in a nice, lean way.

It was great, a solid 8/10. The only thing is halfway through the night I'm talking about my love for a spag-bol and he looks me dead in the eyes and he goes... 'you know I'm vegan'.

This is worse than when my first Tinder date told me, 'if you dropped a stone you'd be a stunner'. It was then that I realised this whole date was pointless. I panicked and downed all four of the shots he'd bought us and told him I needed to go wash my fish and quickly hurried out before he could respond. Safe to say, I was pretty pissed. Why didn't he say that on his profile? Give a girl fair warning, you know? Either way, I'm blocking his number as we speak. I don't have time for that.

The first guy this week though? Prime material. He went by the name of Chad Waller and said he'd take us to a five-star restaurant and treat us to a three-course meal. I was worried when he ordered the vegetarian appetiser. I mean vegetarian wouldn't be the worst thing in the world, but it wasn't really what I was after. But I stuck around and I'm glad I did.

The waiter came to take our order for the mains and he immediately said, 'Medium rare steak'. Jackpot. The waiter turned and asked me what I wanted and in a cute, quiet voice I said, 'just a salad' and looked back down at the table, waiting for Chad to ask me what was wrong. In the corner of my eye, I could see him studying me.

(CHAD)    'You know, I like a girl who looks after her weight. Most women I take here just order the steak as well and I always think, don't you have enough meat *on* you, am I right?'

LENA      He chuckles nervously and I flash him a confused look before getting all sad and cute again.

'I don't really understand what you mean.' I mumbled. There's a long pause as I wait for him to take the bait.

(CHAD)    'Did I... did I do something?'

LENA      And there it is. 'Well... sort of.'

| | |
|---|---|
| **(CHAD)** | 'Well, what? What is it?' |
| **LENA** | 'I just... I just don't really understand how you could just order a steak like that, you know? Right in front of me, like... like it's nothing.' |
| **(CHAD)** | 'I'm not quite sure what you mean.' |
| **LENA** | 'Chad. Have you ever seen Cowspiracy?' |
| **(CHAD)** | 'Oh Jesus Christ, that's it. I'm leaving.' |
| **LENA** | He gets up to leave and I suddenly panic. This was not part of the plan. |
| | 'Wait, Chad, just wait. If you stay, then you might get more meat than you bargained for tonight.' |
| | I can hardly believe the words coming out of my own mouth and my god do I feel cheap. But I knew it's what I had to do. |
| **(CHAD)** | 'I'm listening.' He slowly sits down and I look him dead in the eyes. |
| **LENA** | 'Did you know that 2,400 gallons of water are needed to produce one pound of beef. Eating one fewer pound of beef saves as much water as not showering for six months.' |
| **(CHAD)** | 'This is bullshit...' |
| **LENA** | He gets up to leave again so I quickly grab his hand and put it on my boob. |
| | 'More than six million animals are killed for human consumption every hour. In one lifetime, the average American will consume the equivalent of 11 cows, 27 pigs, and 2,400 chickens.' |

The boob thing seemed to work so I grab his other hand and do the same thing.

'Animal agriculture alone is responsible for 18% of global climate change. That's more than all forms of transportation combined. Globally, cows produce 150 billion gallons of methane per day, which is twenty-five to a hundred times more destructive than $CO_2$.'

We're breathing hard and staring into each other's eyes and we stay like that until we hear an awkward cough next to us.

(WAITER)  'Sorry to interrupt but your food, sir and... madam.'

LENA  'Yes, right.' Chad says, slowly removing his hands from my chest and watching as the steak is placed under his nose. He looks at it and I look at him and the waiter looks at me and then we both look at him and then he looks at the waiter and says... 'I've changed my mind. I think I'll just have the salad as well.'

Victory!

After the salad and dairy-free sorbet for dessert, he asks me if I want to go back to his, but I don't really see the point seeing as my work here is done. But I do let him kiss me and tell him to text me, just so, you know, I can keep tabs on whether he's plant-based for the long-run and not just for tonight.

I've got another date this evening. I know this one definitely won't be a waste of time because I've already stalked his Insta and found several food pics starring chicken and fish. If this one goes well he'll be the fourteenth guy I've turned vegan this month.

Seven o'clock rolls around and I'm sat at the bar, going over the lines in my head with some new facts I'd Googled this morning. The guy I matched with is called Lark Sparrow and the second he walks through the door I know exactly why. He's wearing loose cargo trousers that look like they're three sizes too big and a huge brown and green poncho and that wasn't even the worst part. The worst part... was the man bun. He spots me immediately and swaggers over, taking his sweet time as I awkwardly sit there just staring at him. After what feels like hours, he finally approaches me.

**(SPARROW)**    'You must be Lena, huh? The name's Sparrow.'

**LENA**        Oh lovely, a grown man who goes by his fake last name. He puts his fist out to bump mine, but I panic and just cover his hand with my palm.

'Hi... Sparrow. So, shall we grab something to drink before we head into the restaurant?'

**(SPARROW)**'Sure thing, yeah. I'll just have an apple juice thanks.'

**LENA**        An apple juice? Oh god, so the guy wasn't even gonna get drunk. This was gonna be a tough cookie to crack. I figure I may as well just cut to the chase.

'So, Sparrow. You look... very um... vegan.'

(**SPARROW**)     'Vegan? Me? Oh no no, I live off the fatta the land. My dad owns a farm so we kill all our chickens ethically.'

**LENA**        Thank god.

'Ah. Love me some ethical killing.' He doesn't laugh. He receives his apple juice but doesn't give it a second look because he's just... staring at me.

'Are you okay?' I ask.

'Yeah. Yeah.' He says slowly, nodding. He's starting to look me up and down and I begin to wonder whether this one would even be worth the hassle.

'Where'd you get that top?'

'Topshop.'

I feel confused. He nods.

(**SPARROW**) 'Did you know, nearly 70 million barrels of oil are used each year to make the world's polyester fibre, which is now the most commonly used fibre in our clothing. But it takes more than two hundred years to decompose.'

**LENA**        'What the hell...?'

(**SPARROW**) 'Globally, we now consume about 80 billion new pieces of clothing every year−400% more than we were consuming just two decades ago.'

**LENA**        'I should go.' I get up to leave but he grabs my hand and puts it on his chest. I'm about to pull away but under the poncho he's kind of muscly. So I let him.

**(SPARROW)** 'Nine out of ten workers interviewed in Bangladesh cannot afford enough food for themselves and their families, forcing them to regularly skip meals, eat inadequately, or go into debt.'

**LENA** He's gasping and we're staring into each other's eyes and the tension is as raw as Chad's steak and before I know it we're kissing, apple juice flying off the counter, my hands in his man bun and at this point, I don't even know what's skin and what's poncho. After what feels like a full minute, we break away. In my peripheral, people are staring at us but I don't care. I manage to gather enough breath to speak.

'Tom. Shit, I mean Chad. Fuck, I mean Sparrow... you know there's no such thing as ethical killing, right?'

**(SPARROW)** 'I had my suspicions.'

**LENA** My mind is racing and I wonder if I'll regret what I say next.

'Listen, Sparrow. I'll start wearing second-hand ponchos if you go vegan.'

He looks at me in horror and shock before doing one of those weird, hippy, side-smiles.

**(SPARROW)** 'Deal.'

*She looks to the audience.*

**LENA** Victory!

*Lights down.*

## Scene 2. Office.

*Lighting changes to very bright, office environment.*

LENA            It's 9am. I left Sparrow last night shortly
                after our little deal – I didn't much see the
                point in hanging around. I tap my lanyard
                in to access the building and head straight
                for the lift. I work at a call centre. It's not
                my ideal job, no, but it pays the bills. The
                morning team meeting has already started,
                and I quickly rush to join at the back.

                'Right, now that we're all here, let's get
                the nasty stuff out of the way.' Chris-the-
                Manager booms.

                'Number one, whoever has been missing
                the toilet seat needs some serious help. We
                are all adults here and Maria the cleaner is
                this close to quitting, so let's get our shit
                together. Literally. Number two...'

                'You already covered the number two, Sir.'
                A chap called Stephen says next to me.
                Hushed chuckles fill the room before Chris-
                the-Manager tells everyone to be quiet.

(CHRIS)         'Very funny. Number two, sales have been
                down by fifty percent the past week, so
                we'll be adding some new incentives for
                you all... raffle tickets.'

*Chris stands waiting for a reaction from his employees, disappointed by their lack of response.*

'Right, back to your computers and as always, come to me with any questions!'

**LENA** Everyone shuffles their wheely chairs back to their stations and I do the same.

'Raffle tickets huh.' Stephen pipes up next to me. 'What a joke.'

My first call comes through and I can see Stephen dejectedly swivel his chair back into his booth.

'Hello?'

'Hi Mrs Dolores, this is Lena calling from *Your Horse.*'

**(DOLORES)** 'Buttercup?'

**LENA** 'No, no, not *your* horse. *Your Horse*, the magazine you subscribed to.'

**(DOLORES)** 'Oh god not you again, what the shit do you want?'

**LENA** 'I was just wondering if you knew about the ethics of Ascott?'

**(DOLORES)** 'I don't care...'

**LENA** 'Did you know that racing exposes horses to significant risk of injury and sometimes death through trauma or emergency euthanasia.'

**(DOLORES)** 'Oh for crying out...'

**LENA** 'Racing involves striking the horse with a whip to enhance performance, which inflicts pain, and can result in injur...'

The phone line goes dead before I can finish.

'Lena.' Chris-the-Manager booms. 'My office. Now.'

I sigh and pull the headset off, trotting over to the door he was angrily holding open for me. Chris has called me in for a 'meeting' every day since I started working here. So, roughly five times now.

'Listen, Chris-the-Manager, I can explain...'

'Will you stop calling me that, my name is Chris, just Chris. And will you take that ridiculous poncho off, you're distracting the entire office.'

'I actually think you'll find it'll be more distracting with it off.'

| | |
|---|---|
| **(CHRIS)** | 'Just do as I say.' |
| **LENA** | I pull the poncho off in one sweep and sit there in nothing but my jeans and a bra. Chris-the-manager looks at me in horror and disgust before sighing in defeat. |
| **(CHRIS)** | 'Lena.' |
| **LENA** | 'Just Chris.' |
| **(CHRIS)** | 'You have been hired to sell magazines, yes?' |
| **LENA** | 'Oui.' |
| **(CHRIS)** | 'And have you been selling magazines?' |
| **LENA** | '...Yeah.' |
| **(CHRIS)** | '...okay, fair point, but have you also been scaring customers away with what you like to call 'horse activism'?' |

| | |
|---|---|
| **LENA** | 'I'm not scaring anyone away, I'm enlightening them.' |
| **(CHRIS)** | 'Yes, well, enlightening is frightening.' |
| **LENA** | Chris took a quick pause to bathe in pride for coming up with his little rhyme before continuing. |
| **(CHRIS)** | 'Either way, this is your last warning.' |
| **LENA** | 'You said that last time.' |
| **(CHRIS)** | 'Out!' |
| **LENA** | I sigh and roll my eyes, swinging the door open and sauntering out. I hear a few gasps coming from around the office. |

'Poncho!' Chris yells, throwing it in my direction. I grab it and shimmy it on, heading back to my seat.

'Nearly fired again?' Stephen said.

'How'd you guess?' I said. I was about to turn away when I suddenly saw... was that... a cheese string on Stephen's desk? Bingo.

'Stephster...you know, I've actually been meaning to ask you, if you wanted to come to a family dinner tomorrow? I feel like we've really connected over the past... few minutes and it's probably time you meet the parents.'

Usually, I would know better than to scare a man away with the prospect of family dinners, but Stephen looked like the kind of guy whose mother was always begging him to get a girlfriend so she could have grandkids.

'That sounds fun.' He smiled. I guessed correctly.

I got home to my apartment, hung up my poncho, showered, fed all the random stray cats that live in the alleyway and made myself a pot noodle. I switched on Netflix and watched 'Okja' for the fiftieth time whilst brainstorming how I could attempt to convert my family again at this dinner tomorrow. Somehow, the men who knew nothing about me were simply easier to persuade than the family who'd known and loved me from birth.

*Lights down.*

## Scene 3. Family Dinner

*Outside family home, suburbs.*

LENA    It's 6pm and I'm at my parents' house, Stephen at my side. The large, familiar doors loom over me and I suddenly think about turning back. My parents are pretty well off, hence the three-storey house. My mother opens the door, vodka tonic in one hand and her tiny Pomeranian called Mozart in the other.

'Darling, hello.' She coos, kissing me on both cheeks like I was some kind of fancy

European guest whilst completely ignoring Stephen.

'What's with the poncho?'

'It was a trade thing... are you gonna let me in?'

**(MUM)** 'Still haven't learnt any manners I see. I don't know how you think you'll get a husband with an attitude like that.'

**LENA** 'I literally have a guy next to me.' I say, stepping into the high ceilinged hallway, pushing my shoes off at the door. I plod into the dining room where my father is sat with a newspaper.

'Hello Maralena,' he says, without looking up.

'Ugh please don't call me that, Lena will do.'

'**(DAVID)**!' mum screams up the stairs.

'WHAT?' David screams back.

**(MUM)** 'COME DOWNSTAIRS, YOUR SISTER'S HERE.'

**(DAVID)** 'UGHH.'

**LENA** As you can guess, David is my brother. David is unemployed, lives at home and is even more of a bachelor than I am. David comes plonking down the stairs, a disgusted look on his face like he'd smelled a bad fart.

'Hi David.' I say. He grunts in response.

As soon as we sit down at the table, the doorbell rings and doesn't stop ringing. More relatives filter through; my mum's uptight sister with her husband and their four kids, which is four too many if you ask me and my senile grandmother, who usually just sits at the end of the table muttering unintelligible things about the war. Once we'd all settled around the table, my aunt immediately starts interrogating Stephen about his yearly income. I turn to my brother.

'So David, how's the music career coming along?'

**(DAVID)** 'Firstly yeah, it's MC Cold Hustle to you. Secondly, you can give it a rest with the sarcasm.'

**LENA** 'And you can give it a rest with the fake gangsta voice. You're thirty-seven.'

David quit school at seventeen to pursue a music career, or as he likes to call it, 'making beats'.

'So, MC Cold Hustle, can I hear your latest "beat"?'

'David, where the hell did you get those earrings?' My mother suddenly screamed. 'And when did you even pierce your ears?'

David took a deep breath.

**(DAVID)** 'How many times woman? I'm not David. I'm M.C. Cold. HUSTLE. And the earrings are none of yo bizz.'

**(MUM)** 'You stole them didn't you?'

**LENA** My mother was seething at this point and definitely drunker. I sit back, enjoying the show. David kisses his teeth.

**(DAVID)** 'No.'

| | |
|---|---|
| **(MUM)** | 'Yes. Yes you did.' |
| **LENA** | Mum grabs his ear, inspecting the jewellery. 'These are goddamn Cartier, there's no way you could afford this! You're a goddamn disgrace.' |
| | 'Yeah well when I'm rich and famous from my beats, I ain't buying you nothing. No house, no car, nothing.' He said, starting to thump back up the stairs. |
| **(MUM)** | 'Oh get your head out of your arse, David.' |
| **(DAVID)** | 'I ain't David, you bitch!' |
| **(DAD)** | 'David!' My father yelled. |
| **(DAVID)** | 'I hate you all.' |
| **LENA** | We hear his door slam at the top of the stairs. There's a heavy silence. My mum slowly turns back around to face the room. |
| **(MUM)** | 'Sorry about that everyone.' |
| **LENA** | She knocks back the rest of her drink. 'Now, who wants canapés.' |

*Stephen raises his hand.*

| | |
|---|---|
| **(STEPHEN)** | 'I do.' |
| **LENA** | As the atmosphere went somewhat back to normal, I head over to where the kids are playing in the corner of the massive dining room. There'll be more sanity here than with anyone else in this room. |
| | 'Hey guys.' I say softly. 'What books did mummy and daddy give you there?' |
| | I glance over at the books and toys spread out on the floor... all of them splashed with happy looking cartoon animals. |

'I have a better story than any of those.'

Their eyes all light up and they stare at me, waiting.

'There once was a cow called Mary. Mary lived on McDonalds farm but she didn't like it there. They kept her tied up to a metal bar and she couldn't move anywhere or talk to any of the other cows. Then one day, the farmer came along and shoved a big metal pole right up Mary's bum! A few days later, Mary got pregnant. Mary was so excited to finally be having a baby, but when the baby was born, they kidnapped it and started using all of her baby's milk to feed all the children in the village. Mary got very sad and stopped making milk because she knew her baby wasn't coming back. Then, the farmer grabbed her and took her away to a place where they kill cows that don't make milk! He grabbed a huge axe and...'

'What the hell is going on.' My uncle booms behind me. His voice startles the children and their already distressed faces burst into sobs. I turn around, ready to defend myself before I suddenly see my mother carrying a whole chicken to the table.

'Mum what the hell, I thought we agreed on getting a tofurkey...'

'Yes, well I changed my mind. Deal with it.'

She spits. I can feel the anger boiling inside me. My gran starts muttering things to herself, adding to the noise that was fast growing around us.

'How would you like it if I cooked Mozart and served him to the family, huh?' I said, placing him on the table next to the chicken, trying to prove a point. 'Look, he's about the size of it too!'

'Why are you still clinging on to this stupid animal rights' shit.' My mum screams.

'Stupid animal rights' shit? What are you, a psychopath?'

'NAZI.' My gran suddenly yells whilst pointing at me. 'NAZI.'

My mum jumps back in, ignoring her.

'Oh you're just a waste of fucking space Lena... I wish I had aborted you.'

*Pause.*

The kids stop crying. My gran stops screaming. Mozart miraculously stops barking. Everything is suddenly still as my mother's words hang in the air.

I gently pick up Mozart. Every eye in that room is fixed on me and hard as stone. I grab my bag and shove my shoes on, heading out the door for what I decided was the last time.

*Lights down.*

## Scene 4. Tarquin.

*Inside apartment.*

**LENA**　　　When I got back to my apartment, I plopped Mozart on my lap and immediately started flicking through Tinder. If my family won't respect me, then I'm sure some random dude on the internet will. I swiped right on every man that popped up; be them tall, short, fat, skinny, married. No stone left un-turned, no man left un-vegan. I was mid-swipe when I saw absolute gold flash up on my screen. It was a guy who went by the name of 'Tarquin von Farage', proudly standing with a gun in both hands and one foot on a dead bear.

*She puts her hands together in a prayer and looks up to the sky, mouthing, 'thank you.'*

　　　　　　　I mean, the guy may as well have been standing there with his micro-penis in hand. I bet he rides a really loud motorbike too. I started flicking through more of Tarquin's pictures. There was one with his hands round the necks of two pheasants, one with his burly dog standing next to him with a fox in his mouth, even one with him standing over a very endangered and very dead Bengalese tiger. I mean, this was the worst kind of human and oh boy, did I like a challenge.

'So rare to see a real man on one of these apps.' I typed. 'I'm sure that tiger isn't the only pussy you could destroy.'

God I hate myself sometimes.

'My gun is pretty big.' He replied. 'Loaded with bullets too.'

'Maybe I could wear my leopard print leotard and you can chase me around the house with your big gun.'

**(TARQUIN)**  'Only as long as you're running on all fours.'

**LENA**  'Tomorrow. Your place?' I replied, hoping to end this conversation before I threw up.

**(TARQUIN)**  'Perfect. Come at one. You're the only meal I'll be having for lunch.'

**LENA**  I nearly threw my phone across the room. This had better be worth it.

'Yummy. Send me your address.'

*She changes into a leopard print leotard, a large fluffy jacket and leopard print ears.*

Tarquin lived a twenty-minute walk from me. The place was huge and of course, gated. There was a monitor by the side of the gate, with the words 'The Farage's Manor' engraved above it. I pressed the button.

**(TARQUIN)**  'Lena! My sexy minx, do come in.' There was a buzz and the gate popped open. I tentatively walked in, past the fountain and several Aston Martins, straight to the porch. The door opened.

'Oh wow.' Tarquin stood there, one hand on the doorway, the other on his hip. 'Well, you look nothing like your pictures... come in.'

**LENA** 'Thanks.' I said, popping Mozart down and letting him run into the house.

**(TARQUIN)** 'Oo bought us a pup to kill?' Tarquin snorted.

**LENA** 'Now, now, don't get any ideas.' I joked, despite my genuine concern for what he'd just said.

I shut the door behind me and walked down the hallway, my amazement building as I moved further into the largest living room I'd ever seen in my life. The ceilings had no end to their height and as for the walls... they made me want to throw up more than the disgusting texts from last night. Every inch was covered in dead animals. Animal skin, animal heads, animal tusks... I wanted to mount Tarquin's head on a plank of wood and see how he likes it.

'Wow, this is... quite something.'

**(TARQUIN)** 'Isn't it just?'

**LENA** He made a weird growling sound that I think was supposed to be sexy, before he started slowly prowling towards me.

'So Tarqy, what got you into hunting?'

*She dodges him.*

**(TARQUIN)** 'Oh, you know. How most young boys get into hunting. To impress the ladies haha!'

| | |
|---|---|
| **LENA** | He went to go and touch my waist, but I quickly backed away, turning to face a giant polar bear head roaring in my face. |
| | 'Oh really? I thought proper ladies don't like violence.' I walked further away, acting like I was interested in his dead head collection. |
| **(TARQUIN)** | 'Well, uh well... real men...' He stuttered, following me. |
| **LENA** | 'Well, you know what they say about men that hunt, right?' |
| **(TARQUIN)** | 'And what's that, my little tiger?' He started growling and went to playfully pounce on me but I dodged him once again by heading towards a stuffed penguin. |
| **LENA** | 'Well, it's a well-known fact in the... female community, that men who hunt are trying to compensate for... you know...?' |

*He grunts.*

| | |
|---|---|
| **(TARQUIN)** | '...Really?' |
| **LENA** | 'Yeah.' I nodded, knowing I had him somewhat caught in my snare now. |
| | 'There's actually a whole forum about it. On Reddit. It's just a bunch of ladies... hot ladies too... who just talk about how pathetic it is when a man shoots and guts and skins a defenceless...' |

*She becomes childlike.*

'...little wittle baby?'

Tarquin's brows were furrowed as he gazed out the window. I could practically see the cogs turning in his brain.

**(TARQUIN)** 'B...b...but... you told me it was rare to find a real man on Tinder.'

**LENA** Dammit. He started prowling towards me again. I was about to say something else when Tarquin whipped out a leopard tail from his jacket.

*Tarquin produces a leopard tail with a butt plug attached to the end.*

I was suddenly backed up against a stuffed warthog and realised I was in too deep.

*Lena begins to imitate a phone ringing.*

'Oh god, wait, is that my phone?'

*She picks up the phone.*

'Hello? Chlamydia? Oh my god!'

*She mouths to Tarquin.*

'So sorry!

'Yep... yep... okay... bye now. Wow I'm so sorry Tarquin, I have to go.'

I quickly ducked under his arm and grabbed Mozart. 'Let's continue this next week, okay? Sorry again.' And with that, I hurried out the door.

*Lights down.*

## Scene 5. Intervention.

*Inside apartment.*

**LENA**          As I paced back down the road, I wondered if Tarquin would question the toxic micro penis masculinity motivations behind his hunting hobby. Hopefully he'll just stick to bird shooting for now. I finally got back to my apartment, and I went to put my keys in the door but realised it was... unlocked. Tentatively, I opened the door.

'Hello? ... I have a very vicious guard dog with me and I'm not afraid to use him.'

Silence. I round the corner into the living room and sat around the sofas and chairs were my fourteen conquests from the past month.

'What... the fuck!' I say slowly.

'Lena,' Stephen stands up, clearly the spokesperson of the group. 'I'm glad you're here.'

'How'd you get into my apartment?'

**(STEPHEN)**   'Well, you see, Daniel had a key...'

**LENA**          'Who the hell is Daniel?'

*A small, ginger-haired man shyly raises his hand.*

**(STEPHEN)**   'A guy you went on a date with last week. He said you liked him so much, you gave him a spare key when you were drunk.'

**LENA**          Sounds like me.

'Okay, and can I ask what you're all doing here? Together?'

**(STEPHEN)** 'Well, Lena. This is an intervention. Chad, take it away.' Stephen sits down and I look at the man who stands up.

**LENA** 'Lena,' Chad starts, putting down his briefcase.

**(CHAD)** 'When I first met you, I thought you were a charming, young girl. A bit of a wildcard, but charming, nonetheless. When you expressed your passion to me about salads and Cowspiracy, I couldn't help but be taken aback by the sheer fervour you exuded, leading me to be convinced by your arduous argument. However, when I didn't get a text back, I was shocked. Confused. Nay, upset. Then to hear that I was merely game for you to hunt, well, that really was the cherry on the Victoria sponge.'

**LENA** 'Victoria sponges don't have cherr... wait so you're all here because you're annoyed that I didn't text you back? How did you even find each other in the first place?'

**(BLOND GUY)** 'Well, actually...' This time it was some blonde hunk speaking. 'There's a facebook page about you. It's called, "Lena's a manizing danger to mankind and will take away your manhood and meat, don't fall for it, rise up against this vegan witch."'

**LENA** I stand there as I wait for this all to sink in.

'Okay, wow. I'm sorry you're all so weirdly hurt by this but it's not like any of us actually properly dated. The closest thing I got to a relationship was probably Sparrow and that's only because we kissed, but again that was one time.'

Murmurs filled the room as a few people turned to Sparrow.

'Silence! Stop. Stop. I want everyone out. Come on, get out. I'm not dealing with this.' I grab my broom and start trying to shoo them out the door.

'We're not animals, Lena.' Sparrow speaks for the first time.

**(SPARROW)** 'We're not leaving until you hear every single one of us out.'

**LENA** I look around the room. Their desperate eyes were all fixed on me.

'Okay fine.' I sigh. 'But first things first.'

I grab a pen.

'I'm gonna need to number you all so I know who's who.' I went around the circle and wrote numbers ranging from one to fifteen on their foreheads and then sat back down.

'Okay, uh, number twelve. Take the stage.'

The general consensus was every guy was annoyed because they felt I'd used them. Although Sparrow seemed genuinely upset we weren't going to spend the rest of our lives together wearing ponchos and raising chickens. Everyone said their piece until it was only Stephen left.

**(STEPHEN)** 'Lena. Ever since you started working at the call centre seven days ago, I've liked you. I thought you were interesting. Wild. Maybe a little crazy. But I always admired you from afar. You never had any interest in me. So you can only imagine my surprise when you suddenly decided to speak to me two days ago. Little did I know, it's all because you must've seen that cheese-string on my desk. That damn cheese-string. I should've known you were never really after me. The next series of events will shock you all. One, you invite me to a family dinner with only a day's warning. Two, I find out you bring a new man to your family home every week. Three, you leave me at the family dinner with no way home. Four, I find this facebook page when I typed your name into the search bar, hoping I could send you a friend request. You can imagine my shock. Lena, I say this from the bottom of my heart. You are... a bitch.'

**LENA**    He sits down, his face the colour of a beetroot and his hands shaking. I could almost swear I saw a tear in his eye.

'Okay, well, thank you Stephen for that end note. Well, once again, I am very sorry I caused everybody so much upset, that wasn't my intention, believe me. I hope you all found this evening to be somewhat cathartic for you. And hey, at least we're all vegan now. So some good has come of this.'

**(SIX)**    'No, fuck that.' Number six stood up. 'Why would we be vegan knowing that's all you wanted from us. Come on guys.'

**LENA**    The group all started to murmur in agreement, gathering their things.

'Wait, what? What do you mean?' I tried to stop each one at the doorway to reason with them, but they were all forcefully pushing past. I stood there, watching as the men all left. It was like watching every glimmer of hope and effort I'd made over the past month just disintegrate. I felt a tap on my shoulder.

**(TOM)**        'Lena.'

**LENA**         I looked at him blankly.

**(TOM)**        'I'm Tom... The vegan... Number 12?'

**LENA**         'Right... yes, sorry. Been a long day. What did you want?'

**(TOM)**        'Here.' He handed me a flyer. 'I conduct marches and rallies for animal rights. Our next one is actually tomorrow. Might be a slightly better-slash-more effective form of activism than this. Although I admire the creativity.'

**LENA**         I looked down at the pamphlet. There were graphic pictures of chickens trapped in cages and pigs being beaten. Just my cup of tea.

'I'll think about it.' I said, playing it cool although unsure as to why.

**(TOM)**        'Great. Maybe see you then.' He saluted and headed out the door as I watched after him, amazed that I'd been on a date with this guy and dismissed him so quickly. I was about to close the door when a figure suddenly leapt out in front of me.

'What now! ... Wait, David?'

**(DAVID)**      'Nah fam, it's not David, it's...'

**LENA**         'MC Cold Hustle, yeah I know, I know. What are you doing here?'

| | |
|---|---|
| **(DAVID)** | 'Came to collect the dog innit.' |
| **LENA** | 'Oh, right. You're not here to see me then?' |
| **(DAVID)** | 'Too many beats to make, too little time.' |
| **LENA** | He shrugged, taking Mozart in his arms. |
| **(DAVID)** | 'Wagwan lil sis.' |
| **LENA** | And with that he swaggered off down the road, little Mozart at his side. I was more sad to see the dog go than my own brother. |
| | I looked back down at the pamphlet Tom had given me. I needed a cathartic few hours of screaming. |

## Scene 6. Protest.
*Street demonstration with crowd.*

| | |
|---|---|
| **LENA** | When I arrived, there were hundreds of people, all dressed in bright colours and hippy tie dye t-shirts. |
| | 'Hey, you want a poster?' Some guy next to me offered, handing over a sign that said, 'Eat beans not beings.' |
| | 'Thanks,' I said, before he disappeared back into the crowd. The packs of people started slowly moving down the street, waving their signs in the air and chanting. |
| CROWD | 'No excuse, for animal abuse! No excuse for animal abuse!' |

'There you are.' A voice yelled in my ear over the sound. I was so charged from all the shouting that I suddenly panicked and punched the guy's face.

'Tom! Shit, sorry. Are you okay?'

**(TOM)**  'I'll live.' He said, rubbing his nose.

**LENA**  'Oh shit, you're bleeding.'

**(TOM)**  'Oh yeah.' Tom said, looking at the blood that had come off on his hand. 'Hey, wanna see something cool?'

**LENA**  Before I could answer, Tom had darted towards a McDonalds that we had now all stopped in front of. He gathered more blood from his nose to his hand and started smearing it on the shop windows.

'Your burger spills innocent blood!' He screamed, terrifying the customers on the other side of the glass.

I'd never been so attracted to anyone in my life. I suddenly got a rush of adrenaline and ran over to the window next to him, pulling my top down. I shoved my boobs against the glass.

'A mother's milk is for her baby, not your milkshake!' I screamed. I breathlessly looked over at Tom and he was looking back at me. We smiled.

The march went on for hours and we stopped at every fast-food chain we could find. I asked Tom to punch me, so I could get a bloody nose too but for some reason he refused. Finally, the crowd stopped outside the Houses of Parliament. There was a podium set up on the green and someone at the front line of the march took to the stage. Everyone quietened down.

**(SOPHIE)** 'Hello everybody. My name is Sophie. If you're new, welcome. It's a pleasure to have you. If you're not new, welcome back. Today is the day where we give a voice to those who cannot speak. To those who cannot defend themselves. Today is a day where we fight for justice for those who have been beaten, eaten, raped, caged and made to live and die in pain for the sole pleasure of our species. They can't fight for themselves, so we'll fight for them. All our lives we've been pressed with this ideology that animals are not like us. That they are 'beneath' us. Despite the fact that we all breathe, eat, smell, walk, communicate, they apparently lack a brain to think, feel, be aware. It's illogical and quite frankly, insane. We're raised on adverts that tell us to have cheese, meat, beef on your chicken, camembert on your pork and then we're asked, 'not feeling so well? Struggling to lose weight? Are you always tired?'

Do you know how much the government profits off of cancer patients? They're killing you. They're killing the animals. And they're killing the environment. It's not enough just putting a badge on your jacket saying, "I heart animals". It's not enough just ranting about how unfair it is with the people that already agree with you. We have to do more. We have to keep

|        |                                                                                                                                                                                                                                                                                                                                                                                           |
|--------|--------------------------------------------------------------------------|

these marches going, we must support every protest we can, stand outside every Canada Goose, pull down every hunting tower, be there to divert every truck that enters those slaughterhouses. It won't be easy. But it will be worth it.'

**LENA**       Sophie stepped down from the podium and the audience erupted in applause. I felt something wet on my cheek and touched my face to feel that it was... a tear. It was the most relief I'd felt in a year. To be surrounded by people who don't keep telling me I'm crazy, to be actively supported in everything I believe in without being shut down or cut off...

'You okay?' Tom asked.

'Yeah, yeah.' I said. 'I miss Mozart.'

**(TOM)**     'Me too. He was a great composer.'

**LENA**      'He sure was. Shall we go back to yours?'

**(TOM)**     'Actually, I'm going to a farm tonight to rescue some chickens. Wanna come?'

**LENA**      I answered him with a very passionate kiss.

*Lights down.*

## Scene 7. Fired and Eviction.
*Bright lights. Interior Office.*

LENA         The next day, I stumbled into the call centre, late and sleep deprived. Tom and I had rescued fifteen whole chickens the night before, which is more exhausting than you'd think. The morning meeting was already in full swing, so I rocked up at the back. Stephen wouldn't even look me in the eye.

'Okay, uh, meeting over everyone.' Chris-the-Manager announced. 'Lena, my office. Now.'

Here we go again. I trundled into Chris's office and sat down on the couch.

(CHRIS)      'Lena, I have tried and I... Wait, is that...? Is that shit on your shirt?'

LENA         I looked down, perplexed.

'Oh yeah.' I chuckled and shook my head, brushing it off.

Chris looked like he was about to say something then changed his mind.

(CHRIS)      'You're being fired.'

LENA         'What? Is this about the horse activism? Because if so...'

(CHRIS)      'It's not about the horse activism, Lena, it's about the... sexual harassment complaints.'

| | |
|---|---|
| **LENA** | 'The what?' |
| **(CHRIS)** | 'A worker whom I cannot name has filed for... a restraining order against you.' |
| **LENA** | I looked out the window into the office and saw... Stephen. Sat there staring at me with an evil smirk on his face. He took a huge bite out of a cheese string. I wanted to say something, but it was clear Chris had made up his mind. With a daze, I did my walk of shame out of the office, trying my hardest to not look back. |

I got back to my apartment and went to open the door to find that it was unlocked... Oh god, not again. I braced myself. I stormed into the living room, ready to tell a plethora of angry men to go home but instead I saw... a letter. It was the fifteenth one of these this month... very official looking, with the words, 'URGENT' in bright red capital letters. I opened it up.

'Dear Maralena Morgan,

We are informing you that your tenancy has not been paid for in the past five months and your lease is up. You have 24 hours until you are officially evicted.'

I picked up my phone. What I was about to do was an absolute last resort, but it had to be done.

*Lena holds her phone to her ear for a second before we hear an automated voice say, 'Your contact named, 'My shitty mother,' has blocked you.'*

I scrolled through my contact list, wondering who I could call. 'Conquest 23...

conquest 55...' conquest this, conquest that... Tom.

*She holds the phone to her ear.*

He picks up on the third ring.

'Tom! Hi. It's me... Lena... I was wondering what you're up to tonight?'

**(TOM)** 'Lena! Hey. I'm actually getting an early night, gotta be up at five tomorrow to try and stop the trucks outside the slaughterhouse. Wanna come?'

**LENA** 'God you turn me on. I'm on my way.'

I shoved a few clothes in a box and hurried out the door. I've decided that I won't tell Tom I'm technically homeless, but just end up staying over indefinitely. When I got to his, he stood in the doorway, wearing nothing but some pants, a t-shirt that said 'Vegan from my head tomatoes.'

'Nice shirt.' I said.

**(TOM)** 'Thanks. Why do you have...?'

*He gestures to the box.*

**LENA** 'I... have a lot of things.'

He looked at me for a moment, perplexed, before shrugging his shoulders.

**(TOM)** 'Cool. Come on in.'

**LENA** I walked into a tiny studio apartment. The walls were filled with PETA posters and there was a giant calendar above his bed. I walked over to it.

'Vegan march, chicken rescue, slaughterhouse protest...' Every day was filled with some kind of activist event.

|          | 'Tom, how do you have the time to do all this? Like, how do you pay rent?' |

**(TOM)**     'Sell the green.'

**LENA**      He whips out a small packet of weed from his pocket.

**(TOM)**     'You want some pasta?'

**LENA**      Tom and I sat down at his tiny dining room table that was a few feet away from his bed. He made us a spag-bol and we played a drinking game called, 'which celeb is vegan.'

I showed him David's Soundcloud and we drunkenly danced and laughed in his kitchen. And for the first time in ages, I felt really, really... happy.

*Lights down.*

### Scene 8. Tom's arrest.
*A loud sound of a buzzing alarm overhead.*

**LENA**      Tom's alarm squealed in my ear at 5am.

**(TOM)**     'You ready to save some pigs?' He croaked.

**LENA**      'Born ready.' I croaked back.

Tom suggested we grab some whiskey from the corner shop as apparently it helps with the nerves. I told him he was a man after my own heart. We went down to the slaughterhouse and everyone ran to the middle of the road, trying to flag down the first truck. It stopped outside of the slaughterhouse, waiting for the gates to open.

*Sound of screaming animals overhead.*

'Do you hear that?' I turned to Tom in a panic.

**(TOM)** 'I know.' He stroked my hair soothingly. 'I know.'

**LENA** He handed me a bag filled with fruit and water bottles. The pigs were parched, and it felt like I was feeding a baby with the bottle in my hand. Which made it all the worse when the pigs were ripped away from us. I stared at the back of the vehicle, trying not to cry. The last truck of the day charged at us as we stood in the road.

'Fuck off!' The driver screamed at us out of his window.

'Fuck you!' Tom screamed back.

'Tom, don't.' I said, grabbing his arm.

'What'd you say to me?' The driver said, stopping the truck.

**(TOM)** 'Do I need to spell it out, you dumb shit? F, U, C, K...'

**LENA** The driver hopped out of the truck.

**(DRIVER)** 'You wanna say it to my face?'

**(TOM)** 'Y, O, U. FUCK. YOU.'

**LENA** The driver shoved Tom and he stumbled back. The pair began scrapping and rolling about on the floor in the most awkward fist fight I'd seen in my life. Fight Club makes it look so much sexier than it actually is. I darted to the back of the truck and tugged at the fence trying to pull it open. The other activists joined, pulling at the wood until finally, it broke free. I ran over to Tom, who had a black eye and was being restrained by the slaughterhouse workers.

'They've called the police, Lena, run!' He screamed at me.

'Let him go,' I yelled, marching up to the workers.

Within seconds, there were sirens in the distance. The police car pulled up, dodging the pigs that ran about manically in the road. One of the cops comically fell over a pig just as they got out of the car.

In a flash, Tom had kicked the worker holding him down and grabbed my hand, the both of us running as fast as we could down the road. There was a loud sound of buzzing and Tom fell to the ground, convulsing as one of the policemen held a taser to his back. I began screaming at them to let him go but the rest of the feds had already caught up and were handcuffing Tom, dragging him to the police car. Tears streamed down my face as they shoved him into the vehicle. I stood there, staring helplessly as Tom looked at me through the glass, watching as he was torn away from me in front of my eyes. Pigs ran around the road as more police cars drove up to the scene, taking statements and assessing the damage.

I felt like I was underwater or like I was having some kind of fever dream and that I'd wake up in a cold sweat, back in my apartment, in my own bed with Mozart at my feet. In a daze, I picked up Tom's bag that he had dropped in the road and carried myself down the street and back to his apartment.

*Lights down.*

## Scene 9. Finale.

*Inside apartment.*

**LENA**  It's five in the morning. I'd woken up in Tom's empty flat. It's been a month since his arrest and now I'm just counting down the days until his landlord finds a new tenant.

As I'm sat on the toilet, I catch a glimpse of myself in the bathroom mirror. I look pale. Well, paler than usual. There are dark circles around my eyes that I'd never really had before. My hair looks thinner. On my way to the protest, I stopped by a corner shop and used my last fiver to grab the cheapest bottle of whiskey I could find. I had a few swigs to prepare myself for the horror I was about to witness again. After about ten minutes, the first truck came trundling down the street and we all rushed to the side with our fruit and water bottles. Looking into the animals' eyes was the worst thing you could do. It was like you could see their soul. Those glossy, brown eyes that don't look much dissimilar to ours.

'I'm so sorry.' I whispered to one of the pigs I was feeding. I stroked his rough little head and after taking the last bite, he slowly closed his eyes with sudden calm. He was enjoying a scratch on the head in the same way Mozart always did. Suddenly, the truck started revving and the pigs were dragged away from us, off to get dangled upside down and their throats slit.

I walk over to the road where the lorry has just passed and in the distance, I see another one coming. The terrified squeals fill the air but instead of the horror I had been feeling the past year, I suddenly feel... calm. As the lorry neared closer, the activists left the road, but instead of following them, I sat down. I took a deep breath. I thought about my family. How MC Cold Hustle was probably still screaming at my mum down the stairs. Maybe he'll finally finish his EP. I thought about work. How Chris-the-Manager had probably shaved off his bum fluff of a moustache and how their sales had probably increased since I stopped scaring customers away with my 'horse activism'. Maybe Ms Dolores has finally stopped riding Buttercup. I wondered if Stephen would ever find a girlfriend. I thought about all those men I'd been on dates with, who cared enough to come to my house and tell me how they felt. I thought about Tom. How his kindness and fearlessness led *him* to being trapped in a cage. The lorry was getting closer. People started shouting. But I didn't care. I didn't care because...

You win.

*The house lights come up and all the sound cuts. Lena looks directly at the audience members.*

Every single one of you. With your ham sandwiches and leather shoes. I suppose at least I know I tried my best. With every man I tried to convert and every march I screamed at and every rally and... and I wish I could tell every dying animal how sorry I am. I'm so sorry that everything I did just wasn't enough. I take another swig of whiskey and I close my eyes.

*She chuckles.*

I need to stop getting drunk.

*Blackout.*

*The end.*

**THE CONVERT** by Ben Kavanagh
ISBN 978-1-912430-76-5   £9.99

**NEXT LESSON** by Chris Woodley
ISBN 978-1-912430-19-2   £9.99

**CARE TAKERS** by Billy Cowan
9781910798-81-2   £9.99

**BREATHLESS** by Laura Horton
ISBN 978-1-912430-83-3   £8.99

**NOOR** by Azma Dar
ISBN 978-1-912430-72-7   £8.99

**THE MAKING OF A MONSTER** by Connor Allen
ISBN 978-1-912430-85-7   £8.99

**FREE-FALL** by Ashwin Singh
ISBN 978-1-911501-07-7   £8.99

**THREE WOMEN** by Matilda Velevitch
ISBN 978-1-912430-35-2   £9.99

**PROJECT XXX** by Kim Wiltshire & Paul Hine
ISBN 978-1-906582-55-5   £8.99

**COMBUSTION** by Asif Khan
ISBN 978-1-911501-91-6   £9.99

**DIARY OF A HOUNSLOW GIRL** by Ambreen Razia
ISBN 978-0-9536757-9-1   £8.99

**SPLIT/MIXED** by Ery Nzaramba
ISBN 978-1-911501-97-8   £10.99

**THE TROUBLE WITH ASIAN MEN** by Sudha Bhuchar, Kristine Landon-Smith and Louise Wallinger
ISBN 978-1-906582-41-8   £8.99

More great plays at:
**www.aurorametro.com**